Cage of Water

Akron Series in Poetry

Also by Author

Message to Be Spoken into the Left Ear of God
Detail from The Garden of Earthly Delights
The Rain That Falls This Far
The Attraction of Heavenly Bodies

Akron Series in Poetry

Elton Glaser, Editor

Barry Seiler, *The Waters of Forgetting*
Raeburn Miller, *The Comma After Love: Selected Poems of Raeburn Miller*
William Greenway, *How the Dead Bury the Dead*
Jon Davis, *Scrimmage of Appetite*
Anita Feng, *Internal Strategies*
Susan Yuzna, *Her Slender Dress*
Raeburn Miller, *The Collected Poems of Raeburn Miller*
Clare Rossini, *Winter Morning with Crow*
Barry Seiler, *Black Leaf*
William Greenway, *Simmer Dim*
Jeanne E. Clark, *Ohio Blue Tips*
Beckian Fritz Goldberg, *Never Be the Horse*
Marlys West, *Notes for a Late-Blooming Martyr*
Dennis Hinrichsen, *Detail from* The Garden of Earthly Delights
Susan Yuzna, *Pale Bird, Spouting Fire*
John Minczeski, *Circle Routes*
Barry Seiler, *Frozen Falls*
Melody Lacina, *Private Hunger*
George Bilgere, *The Good Kiss*
William Greenway, *Ascending Order*
Roger Mitchell, *Delicate Bait*
Lynn Powell, *The Zones of Paradise*
Dennis Hinrichsen, *Cage of Water*

Cage of Water

Dennis Hinrichsen

The University of Akron Press
Akron, Ohio

Grateful acknowledgment to the editors of the magazines in which the following poems first appeared:

AGNI: "Childhood's Face"; *Alaska Quarterly Review*: "Muse Theory"; *Barrow Street*: "Periodicity:"; *Controlled Burn*: "God's Chromosomes" and "Lead Part & Chlorine,"; *Crab Orchard Review*: "Translations from the Natural World"; *Current*: "Rapture"; *Field*: "Partial Glimpses of the Face of Jesus"; *Notre Dame Review*: "Blue Racer" and "Detail from *The Garden of Delights*"; *Paradidomi Review*: "A Night and a Day of Fever," "Aside," and "Zen Noise, Zen"; *Passages North*: "Song"; *Poetry Northwest*: "At This Moment and at This Moment and at This," "Childhood," "Horse Standing in Sunlight," "Power Surge," "The Wave (Dissected)," and "Working at Children's"; and *Way Station Magazine*: "My Mother Watching My Father Shave," "On a Gift of Flowers Thrown by the Wind or a Young Girl," "What the Shroud Holds," and "Zen Noise, Zen" (reprint).

"Horse Standing in Sunlight" and "The Wave (Dissected)" received the Theodore Roethke Prize from *Poetry Northwest.*

"Partial Glimpses of the Face of Jesus" was reprinted on *Poetry Daily* (http://www.poems.com).

08 07 06 05 04 5 4 3 2 1

All inquiries and permissions requests should be addressed to the publisher,
The University of Akron Press, Akron, OH 44325–1703

Library of Congress Cataloging-in-Publication Data

Hinrichsen, Dennis.
Cage of water / Dennis Hinrichsen.-- 1st ed.
p. cm. -- (Akron series in poetry)
ISBN 1-931968-16-0 (pbk. : alk. paper)
I. Title. II. Series.
PS3558.I546C34 2004
811'.54--dc22

2004021379

Manufactured in the United States of America.
First Edition 2004.

The paper used in this publication meets the minimum requirements of American National Standard for Information Sciences—Permanence of Paper for Printed Library Materials, ANSI Z39.48–1984. ∞

Contents

Part I

Part II

Part III

Part IV

for Teresa

stand tiptoe on the tip of a needle
like a grain of sand flashing in sunlight

—Ikkyū
(translated by Stephen Berg)

Part I

Childhood's Face

When the world comes down to this one dark wood
Before our four astonished eyes . . .
To a beach for two faithful children . . .
To a house of music, for our clear accord . . .
I will find you
—Arthur Rimbaud, "Lines"

1. Incantation

Already nostalgia quickens me.
My mother in sunlight as in a yellow rain—
a soft, cotton burnishing—
her forearms, the unblemished silk of catfish hauled from the Cedar.
Loose string in the cables. Loose voltage.
How far fire has to leap along the delicate arc of gasoline before it ignites
the arm.
The sky, a river.
The streets, rivers.
Called out of the creek beds by acres of rust.
I enter by way of my tongue.
Upstream, upwind, splitting grape skins with teeth.
Downstream, the face of the Lord immaculately etched on a crayfish—
a serenity poised between its pin-legged shadow
and on the underside of the water's surface (if this is possible) its mirrored
back.
The third presence calmly siphoning in the heated shallows of a boy's cheek.
Now is windstruck, startled (*the surface ripples*)—gone.
Twigs flensed of their own woven sheathing.
Pollen and paraffin, candle wax.
Dirt under a fingernail as clean as a blade.
A black parenthesis, white parenthesis
(The days, pink grains . . .

2. Memory and Collapse

I can still see her tanned arms turning over and over again to gauge the
tooth-marks,
the impressions (because she beat me), my gift of stones.
Some like rings done laterally to the fingers;
some full strokes, parallel, to the ridge of bone, cut with pressure enough and
kissing, sucking,
to speckle the flesh with blood.

And then a feather, a blue jay's, like a banded flame,
wind high up
in the locusts, the alley
where we wandered, the alley's hedges,
swagged with key rings, shoelace, bracelets of grass . . .

How many nights my name called out from the other side of fences,
how much birdcall in elm,
sunlight bearing down so hard on the pitched roofs it blinded me
as if with broken glass,
its high gloss merging with the glare of the sky—
a connective tissue, an interpretive tissue—
leaf flecks, eye grit—what translates.
So say it again . . .

3. Coda

The boy's face on the water like diaphanous foil or sheeting.
His shadow on the sun-sifted, water-sifted mud, the true measure of daylight's
weight and density.
A bias the birds enter, blackness for blackness

(or mercury for chrome, silver for chrome).
Minnows blistering what is veil-like, curtain, with quick cuts, incessant
    fracturing.
How his mind can hold these things separate:
in the shadow of his face, the shadow of a stone; three grains;
strands of liquid like cool flame sifting from what is permeable, underground.

God's Chromosomes

What can a child know of the skin of daylight, its cell-work
                    as fragrant
          as lilac, warped pliant and soft

in his hands' aimless twisting, the shape of the minutes,
                    the body's progressions,
          drifting, leaf bud and pollen, from the then-thriving

canopy of elm and willow? He is everywhere in daylight
                    a child of God. God's
          chromosomes in starlight: dug-up

worm lengths, bobs and lures, the four-pronged hooks
                    his father gummed
          with catfish paste above the unchained river;

the sound of his voice and his voice's echo
                    the male part and
          the female part; his looking tugged thirty feet up

from a whirlpool . . . To quell this vertigo: the bows
                    of his muddied shoelaces
          slung from their knots. Later, in a night's waking dream

of heaven—a dancer bent in a deliberate calisthenics—
                    the arms, scarves;
          the legs, scarves; everywhere the unimpeachable music

humming its low fire governance. A tattooing
                    that made him rise
          squinting late Iowa mornings, his mother's

younger brother beside him on the cool steps, flesh
                    of his flesh, his own
          skin beside him, feral, electric. What could a child know

of such division and grace? To be crucified in the genes,
                    to hang there—a boy
          in a man's body—*hrsh lght, Gds lght, faltring*

ner th crwn of the skul, as if some fissure had been pinched,
                    had been welded closed.
          Still, their voices threaded. His uncle's,

idiot savant, above his own, detailing by grillwork, by shape
                    of the hood, con-
          figuration of tail lamp, all of creation, God's work,

either (man/child) could be prepared to know: the *whir*
                    of traffic down 22nd Street:
          his uncle separating the Dodges from Chrys-

lers, Chryslers, irrefutably, from late model Pontiacs.

Lead Part & Chlorine,

copper, iron—
tap water I was blessed in—

I do a simple thing
and sluice its

mineral guttings—
my thirst

slaked, my
throat stung

with such
inelegant fiber

and its poor
Jerusalem of fact.

What the Shroud Holds

(Good Friday, 1990)

1.

Pollen of all kinds. Fakery and pigment. Jeweler's
rouge.
Indentations where a man's thumb

pressed down and in to widen gaps
between
the weaving, twenty twists per inch of fiber,

my grandfather laid like soft wax inside the fabric,
his body
even then on the horizontal plane,

en pointe, as if on the plantar nerve,
about to ride
those first anguished seconds

like a bellows. A modesty of crossed hands. Axis
and pivot.
Celestial tinctures. His last

pitched curse flying over the rubber bit—
as the charge
held and the voltage

flashed—to the hovering Jesus.

2.

In Breughel's *The Expulsion*
of the Rebellious

Angels (and could they mean mere
anger
here?), it is a saint cauterizing

the landscape, angels violently poised above
their victims,
nothing scurrying away,

angling for cover, but accepting,
actually helping,
flying into the swords, exposing with delicate

hands their split intestines.

3.

But never
the iridescence I would rub from a moth.

I'd clean the powder with my tongue
sometimes—
he'd watch—just to taste it, or swipe it

in broad strokes on the ball of my wrist—
he'd hone
his jackknife to a keener smoothness,

then peer like me at the assembled
wreckage:
orange bands and yellows of lightning,

crushed reds, some of them marked with star
charts and
the shapes of planets, though now

and then a single butterfly would snap brutally
out of the domestic
ether, flutter across blades of daylight,

so slowly I couldn't help but watch—
he'd be bored
with me by then,

disgusted—a scrap of paper caught in an updraft
or ash
on which I'd seen some writing

floating back
to the barrel edged with fire.

4.

Cross his arms here

so that he might linger in soft
linens
awhile—"Can I get up now?"

"It's over. You're up"—flannel prints, vellums,
human
rapture reduced to this last

cloth touch, ecstasy to this day's end
waking.
He rocks a little in the chair, then moans,

the nurse's voice in his ear like a soreness
or intolerable
law, so he looks at me.

"Can I get dressed now?
                    Can I get ready
          for bed?" I turn in the harsh-threaded

matrix—no vision, no memory, no
                    healing—
          and tell him, "Yes, LeRoy, you can dress."

At This Moment and at This Moment and at This

moment—a pink-gold light
rages at the edge of visible matter,
time spilling

in rods and segments of arcs, curved
as the snow-covered fields
are curved, unmarked

to the edge of infinity. I watch it all
behind
the pitched blade of a windshield,

whatever molecules I've inhaled
and pushed back out—
Christ's tears, ash from a fire—now

oily, smeared: the X-ray of my breathing.
How like vapor
it spikes up to improve its view,

grows six ways at once. All along
the hammered
landscape: ice whiskers and ice teeth.

The trees, too, sheathed in aluminum.
The river
purling in its liquid metal heart.

Each possible union of two things
including now
the deer I saw at dusk,

freshly dying—on its side like a horse,
its body rounded
like a horse—so that I thought it another

creature at first in my swerve
around it;
and this worker, days later,

I saw twisting on the roadside; she, too, freshly
hit, freshly
dying, one leg and part

of her back pinned to the planet,
the other
writhing because something in it had

fractured, her nerves ringing as if touched
by a wire . . .
I say this now because it matters: her

overalls were *rounded, tawny.* Someone
else was out of a car,
screaming across the freeway

to a man on a ladder, who looked away
at first,
and then, with extreme caution, released his hands

from a long parabola of voltage. Sunlight
was every-
where, and a few clouds. A jet,

high up, dropped away from us
like a needle
into a shallow bowl

of milk . . . *Drink,* the gods
instruct us—*at this*
moment—that moment—and in each narrow run *of time—*

Childhood

Sometimes I think I am

already there and memory
just
the crude agent used

to more reluctantly spread
this
wheat-colored shine

(and sometimes I am just downriver
dragging
a stick;

from the wires a bird crying *seek,*
hide-and-go
seek, stay hidden—

high harmonica sheen of the skyline,
a dome,
really, one swart wind leaking,

insignificant, out of a culvert).
Such fine
days, angelic memory.

Wind blurring each pane of glass
with
coagulant rain. A radio

blaring: muse of song, bitch of static.
How raw wood
pierced my tongue

once until what emerged was oak
language,
blood language. My head

in my heart most days, hands scarred
from
where bark had torn me.

I remember pissing now against
a wooden
fence and sucking nails,

rubbing the tip of a monarch's wing
to a saffron
lens, the yard bloodshot,

fractured when I coined my eye:
there,
in simmering daylight,

a child pumped a tire once
until it exploded,
then, thoughtless, idly plucked

the warped spokes until they rang;
the bird
in the apple crying *seek*,

seek, hide-and-go seek; stay
hidden
(the autobiographic:

how the child was happy then
and wasn't
wronged, and not one thing

stirred that was not complete).

Part II

The Wave (Dissected)

                                        is no less remarkable

for its unfocused passion than my fingertips right now
                working a lavender-
        scented lotion onto a woman's back. From

                        the base of the spine,
then up and over knotted vertebrae (touching her rib cage
        with my palms)—my hands,

frangible chalk, sweep in leaflike, fanlike patterns. The
                deep movement
        the same but different—the pressure

                        different—her
response different—my fingertips blown apart to the nothingness
        of spray.

                                        There is no color

for this in the dark, though I say vermilion with an under-
                coat
        of green. Though something

                        pastel-
tinged must linger in the drying lavender streaks—I can feel
                the moisture

wick into the very skin, receptive lateral canvas—
                she's tipped
        on her side—some of the moisture

gone already
to deep water stillness. Now she turns and her throat tightens
blue

at the collar-

bone. Now stirs, and is breath externalized. Curtains
swing a little
in the breeze. Each window

propped
with a slightly curving stick to let more air in, dusk
reduced

to milk cloud and hidden star point. Now a cat
breaks over
the edge of bed and crushes

blankets,
licks at a paw, curls in that zone between the energy
of sleeping

waves—

which cannot touch except through fingertip, that casual
(because
waves are mindless) reaching over

so nipples harden and
belly shines . . . Moonlight
lengthens in the still room, adumbrates what must be

some last wren-shaped fluttering—bird or wind—
                    in down-leaning
          maple: single white arm, tapered ribline, upper

                                    thigh—
one hand slowly churning. Now hair swept up with angular
                    palm-

                                                                    stroke—

neck cords flaring—as if water itself were
                    one part
          wind and this its leaping out in muscular form, fluted

                                    arc,
briefly held instant. I keep my hand at her throat, tran-
          sition,

follow curve, pearled glide of collarbone, more
                    transition, wave
          swell, breathing and then not breathing, and then more

                                    change, tran-
sition . . . Windowpane, flash of traffic, the black air hooding
          it all

with measureless silk.

Zen Noise, Zen

                traffic, my
father sleeps

beneath
a wide-bladed
fan,

head tipped
back, hands crossed
over belly,

bird cry
pouring
out of him

like string
or
knotted rain.

His predicament,
of course,
is time: include

it all, he can-
not
include it all . . .

I let mosquitoes
feed awhile
before I wake him.

Horse Standing in Sunlight

Witless to think such grazing could wound the sun and
yet the sun seems
wounded—late slippage

in a relief of clouds—fence line plunging
the roll
of fields, top wires

edged precisely with sunlight. She makes a knot
of her
face and what lasts is the orbital

twist of lilac, rain's drizzle
on tin
roof, her scent frail as a watermark. Men

sometimes fail miserably at love—in the branched
dark, watery
shadow, legs braid, un-

braid; curtains drift; a column
of thought
folds back on itself like a piece of string

so that no movement forward can undo
its sorrow-
ful gaze—see how the horse stands, claustral,

not one hoof touching the ground—
porous
fluid—

the pasture it hovers in.

Utterly transfixed. The very sign of amplitude,
unbidden
grace, its dun coat

quivering. The sun's eye
in the horse's eye
like ore or nervous water.

Sudden impulse: desires to flee—a blue jay's
shadow
prints its flank with a sharp rip,

black glide, then shreds itself
to rain
in grass top. Downrange, downwind,

out of the field of vision, a spring foal on its side—
all lung and
breath—in a nest of grass. They've gone

back to watch the ballgame finish,
the Amish
women cobalt, orchid, teal, mustard yellow,

pitch and catch. Hard hits to where
the horses stood,
cattle on folded limbs

in a trampled corner. On a rise across the road,
one
horse standing in sunlight.

Fence at its back.

Wind stippling an acre of tree line to whale
skin, a shudder
the oaks

pick up and spread to the river,
the overhanging
willows. She makes a knot

of her thought and strides tidally
into the unwashed
dark, the freshly

mottled bleed-through. Dress, richly colored,
finely
textured. To touch the silence.

Wreckage of grass. That the horse might continue grazing.
Backwash
of teal, orchid, cobalt, burnt

yellows, rain's fine drizzle at daybreak, orbital
twist, a man's face
gone pale as a watermark.

Sudden impulse: but does not flee.
Arms slowly
raised to fence wire: to un-wound the sun.

That the horse might still and the quiet
linger and
the colt awaken and take the apple from her hand.

Blue Racer

Two mules hunkered out of the rain,

though more and more saddled,
raggedly strapped with its curing

leather, a field (not there yesterday) of black-faced
sheep, scrawny
goats—I don't reveal these things

(I see them driving), and yet they drift
in my thought like bits of glass,
reflective shards, as any

thoughts must: spirit rising so surely
out of each spotted
moth, stunted plant,

I would say the sky is curved glass
transcendence bleeds
through (my self curved

glass, bleeding through) . . . More moths and
then the blemishes
in a row of Queen Anne's

lace; a butterfly, red admiral—perfectly
lacquered
wing thrusts, Asian stillness; the carcass

of a dog; wind high up in the limb-thronged
density;
tick of weed stalk, pulverized stone;

the loose, electrical spurts of a swallowtail—more
                    walking, more
          looking—the day again (the day still)

before me—the zone of insects so irrevocably
                    fused with
          bird cry, the succulent flesh of trees,

the very slurs and spears, hidden
                    seams of
          water could be singing.

Where I enter the day—a single blue racer,
                    flattened,
          virus-coiled, I turn with

a stick to peer more closely, to hesitate
                    and probe.
          Like grooves in soft rain, I think: *that snake,*

these scales, the eyes' gaze: uncanny threading.

Rapture

Twilight engendered us, drew us

out of the cool house—where onions,
opalescent
moons, fell apart in phases, our reflections

streaked in the blade's vegetable moistness—
to this other
clarity of thought: six or seven deer

feeding in a field of late summer beans.
No movement
but that of wind thinly stroking

animal presence—our presence—to static
rapture.
The herd sentried,

so it could graze. Our looking
sentried,
cautious. I wanted to reach out and

touch her shoulder as a single fawn
delicately
picked its way downwind to a stand

of trees and an owl (we think)
screamed
once and the field shifted to the deeper

urgencies of night; I wanted words
to have
sway . . . Held breath close

instead. Observed deer.

*

In the kitchen is where
we talk, touch flesh, cooking. Let residues and
sharp herbs

anoint us. The pepper we did not cut
for days
because of its delicate size and washed-out,

pale green coloring—soft rind in scrambled
egg and
sliced tomatoes, cayenne, onion,

crowns of salsa. My hip brushed
hers
when she sliced bread,

crimson robe playing at bare skin—
hers (kinetic),
then mine (domestic) . . . then mine

again. Was this

*

any less rapturous
than her face in my hands in yellowing
light—

smell of emollients, plum rose, coral
shades—
all the contours

and boundaries breaking down
so what I held
was a landscape coming undone,

adding dimension? As air
is
dimensionless

until you notice. As a sheet of river
seems
one thing, then four

or five shades of green.

*

The sky once suddenly
quiet, then brought alive
with swallows

in a rough swerve, kingfishers
circling
tree to wire across the river.

Two males, and then a female—
                        rust-
            marked. A heron's sloppy

wing beats. And then the sun coming
                        out
            in the river's bronzed

heaven, muddied

*

                        golds. I wanted

to reach out and touch her arm,
                        as the boat
            swayed, but could not. Wanted

to say the cranes, quietly feeding,
                        have become
            so tarnished from iron

in the water they do and do not
                        resemble deer . . .
            And then the wind lifted—

I began to speak—the wind touched feathers, skin.

Periodicity:

his forearm

on entering's caught in an animal's mouth, enameled
drag
of instinct. He can feel the ulna

curve
in the hinge of its teeth, as well as bones in his little
finger—such crude

dice—; fat pudge of his thumb's mound. She pries
him loose,
embarrassed—her dog clawing at shirt

tail, uneven
flooring. Hollowness of nine rooms around them, hollowness of
plant stem, empty jars.

Later, pond-life

stirring out of its daze in a one-dimensional shimmer,
their bodies
adrift in a stretch of jazz and soft hips

and posturings
of a sleeping pony. Day's spoke glistening in the wheel
of time.

She bites the cut in his lip—*the sheen of her biting*—
her sentences
in the white air diminished

like temperature
by an order of magnitude: down-angling sparks, the air
a flooding of

clean intent, one wasp under eaves building its nest
in tongue-
lathered spirals.

Periodicity: new day

daylight, imagined columbine, split-petaled azaleas,
the road
to her house doubled on either side with pasture

and Amish
carriage, their free-standing horses—his arm on arriving set again
to the animal's tooth.

Part III

Song

And so then my heart spiked

like a box of Ohio blue tips
I would drag across my pants
or cut with a nail—

always singeing flesh,
the hard button of the wound—
then toss burning so twilight, too,

was ignited for a second
and the water scarred,
Blakeslee shouting *more, more,*

as he tried to set my shirt on fire,
or look for gasoline,
blond sticks collecting downstream to masks
and shields of wicker . . .

I should be less certain now
of many things: the exact line of thought
a bluebird takes

out of the sparse trees to anoint
a fence post and flutter there—
a clipped, cobalt lingering;

or the man flying above the subdivision
in a vehicle no more worthy
than a child's trike,

again and again in a grand design
so that should he plummet
and flail we are his rescue, witness . . .

Good dirt,
the child would say, eating it.
Good river.

The water, when I held it just so,
speckled, shot with strands
and spectrums, exactly like a fish.

Good river, then, finned,
alive in the hand.
The look of a thing stolen:

somebody's prized apples, clusters of grape.
The long scabbed worms
on my thighs and forearms—

where a fence rail
cut them—healing as after a rain.
The feel

of the wounds in the dark like the tapered heads
of matches—
the slow, tentative scratching,

and then the pinprick dots of blood
soaked like sugar into the bedding . . .
No wonder

the days cry out to us in a brilliance of spokes,
                                        the sun
or woman's face, reflected, dreadlocked,

                                        in a dirty window.
A child elsewhere on the soft lawn
                                        watching a honeybee crab-walk

his naked, pale chest, then rest an instant,
                                        thinking to sting—
but never stinging—

                        the banked flesh; the darkening, budding nipple.

Power Surge

What if I said it was ecstasy that caused the outage,
water's dream of becoming light, of becoming nearly
light, finally spitting from the transformer
in a blue haze, the wires gone soft

in a tincture of scalded metal. What if I let this smoke
drift down like a scarf or woman's arm,
the season of thunder and pelting rain
already upon us, *blue herons,*

somebody says, enthralled, *sandhill cranes,*
already the wet earth greening in its re-embrace . . .
That's the trouble with ecstasy. Spring carries it
away. Wind carries it away. We are better

off staying where the ozone lingers,
and the smoke hovers, the woman's hand a slight
pressure in the small of our backs,
making us part of one texture, maybe,

part of one process, as if the very seconds
had come apart to glitter, relaxed, among us—
blue heron, sandhill cranes—our separateness
abandoned to the wreckage and its deepening sigh.

Working at Children's

(Orthopedics, University of Iowa Hospitals and Clinics, 1975)

To look in the patients' eyes was an accomplishment
in those days,
to look deeply and not

turn away, to hold my face so steadily
before theirs
a weld was formed—no matter how far

into illness they had fallen, or how bitter
their exhalations
(always the trace of antiseptics, sour

excrement). Even to offer a kindness,
to find
some joke to break apart the hours;

then later, to cradle an eighty-pound body just returned
from biopsy,
to help sponge the arterial flow.

Oddnesses, daily and everywhere: the diabetic
grinning
as each week they amputated

another jot of leg, the bandaged stump finally swinging
at just above
his knee like a muted bell.

And the woman I startled once as she was dressing,
her nakedness
stunningly green in the fluorescent light,

her neck brace barely able to stem
her hateful glance.
She eventually forgave me—I was an orderly,

after all—and even tipped me
for being kind—
a coil of dollars I took to soothe her

but was too ashamed to count.
It was her back,
a nurse had told, meaning *mind,* then winked.

I winked. The dollars wadded moist,
a spent bandage,
around my keys. And in the children's ward

now and then, miraculously, a child,
broken
by some backward song of the genes,

often tied down and strapped to prevent
an accidental choking.
I held them when I could. I gazed once

into the face of an infant epileptic,
his nearly constant seizure
clouding his astonished eyes.

It amazes me still today how he rocked
and rocked
through it, as if he were possessed

of a beneficent, untranslatable god,
and terror
only what I felt, what I layered over

his incessant shivering. On Ward A,
the hard men
flung from Harleys, jawed like paper cutouts

from pickups and flaming Bonnevilles,
their heads caved in
or rattled silly, each shattered joint

held together with plaster and stainless steel prongs.
Each morning
I'd cross the river

to cart these patients to X-ray or Chemotherapy,
to Sigmoid
or Pulmonary Function,

to have their brains scanned or stomachs probed,
or their entire
bodies flipped and held suspended

while surgeons fed a luminous decay
to their exposed
groins. How they'd bravely press their chests

and lungs into each new machine,
their faces pale,
nearly breathless, and then draw back slumped.

Not only their bodies, but their fluids, too,
I transported
from clinic to clinic: sick blood and urine,

jars of it painfully siphoned
from the viscera.
And each scent vivid

despite the constant mopping. An astringent
iodine,
something rank and viral drying.

The same smells that might have lured Whitman
to bend among
the wounded, the smears of palm-edge,

the hand-grips that ringed my arms, the patients
healing
or sickening regardless, me

entering the well-scrubbed rooms; them gazing
with pain-softened
eyes, hesitant, expectant; then abruptly turning away.

A Night and a Day of Fever

> *Is it in such bottomless nights you sleep, exiled,*
> *O countless golden birds, O Force to Come?*
> —Arthur Rimbaud, "The Drunken Boat"

Late evening, lightning comes and rips the fields. He runs and runs, collects gritty diamonds the size of fingertips—dry ice and volcanic leavings, razored snow that burns him. So what if his father turns rigid with anger at the yard's edge, as raw and angular as a crucifix? The night's hard rain will hammer the glass and soothe the child, its supple continents a skin and mask, and he muttering in German he's sick to his mother: *he's chest deep in a snowdrift/stippled with fever/an arm and a leg of wind/a sleeve of wind/his mother's hand coming down to mop at him with towels and to press his head into the pillows/the April creek gone brilliant with feathers/the swans torn/his own mind torn/the snapper bottom drifting on its gorged heart* . . . In the morning, at the end of the road, he ingests the body and blood of the Lutheran Jesus, then works through the heave of daylight, daylight's crush, the bitter boiling reds of the tractor, the fields turned over to their ridiculous beast. A chicken hawk spills from a phone line, its small fire stoking the ditch grass to pin down one wave of undulant nothingness, then dissolves again—a piece of creek water—back to the sky. The boy pinches a blade of grass, makes it whistle. Waits for his breath to still, to spawn half-pearls along his forehead. For days he has watched his father unrepentant with livestock, or with engines spewing a fine froth, his shirt back mottled to a magnificent leopard—wild eyes and paw prints—one wedge twisting brutally out of the lumbar—*whoosh* of a belt being whipped through loops. The boy's desire now: something clawed, angelic. Landscape dead calm on the skyline. A single red blossom—bruise or welt—that can outlast summer and yet hold its fragrance. And delicate wind, delicate wind always. If there is to be a China on the other side, or compassionate river, it is here in the pitched roofs and silos that flare in the distance—evening pooling green, gray-green, around them—a scatter of crows briefly silvered over ruined corn.

My Mother Watching My Father Shave

She watches him pose as in the commercials,
the lather thick as snow in the curve of his palm,
a dollop he scoops with short, quick strokes—
the fingers stiff, painterly—sideburns to base
of the jaw, narrow chin (the dimple hidden),
his face oddly feminine—(some

water's splashed and clots an eyelash)—
in those bands and swipes of clarity he's toweled
from the mirror. She sings and tugs
at nylons, the motion in her (which is like
forgetting) a gentle swaying as she clears
her head of steam and the room, the song

from last night's television. My father
tips his neck, nicks his throat: *so much brightness*
from a little cut, like a fish's vent below his jawline.
He curses and is like a man adding
numbers or scolding children—a voice
from a well as he dabs with a bit of Kleenex

the still-bleeding wound. What is suddenly real
is daylight. Snow, wind. She slides
a burnt orange stick across a broken nail, then
spreads the still-elegant hands
as in a commercial: the nails glimmer
muted pink in a kind of beginning

glamour, the moons crisp, rising
out of the cuticles. She dreams a little, gazes
at soap. A jar of Ponds unopened; a blue

towel. Done, my father pulls a web of skin
to test its smoothness, then throws
a broken bird of water—two wings—into

his burning face (she thinks: *my pores
must have opened in all this steam*): something bracing,
cold, as invisible as memory—sound
of the jar's lid coming cleanly undone—*two turns
and it is open*—the unblemished ointment strangely
warm and pliant to her digging hand . . .

Muse Theory

It begins as a stone, some pause in the wind I mis-
take for my own
voice calling me back

from wherever my mind took me,
which is the exact
size of a tiny stone—perhaps one

of those stones my wife brings back from the lake
each August
to line her garden—

either way it's space or time, the exact shape
of a man's
body, the space he lives in,

the present moment casting its one coin again
and again
to the perfectly dimensionless

grass. It's one sheet when I look
at it, no
gaps in the weave. The lawn strewn—

because children are reckless.
It begins,
as I said, as a stone which when it moves

is molten. I was born out of a woman's
body, grown
out of a woman's body—

fish body, boy body—so I think I feel it,
the will here
that is measurable in shafts of rain,

pounds of punishing daylight. Some nights—
who can blame me?—
I lie awake and imagine all of human

suffering—sprayed over shattered stonework,
cut streets;
some of it believably jetted—

because the heart is furious, the arteries
furious—;
the visible stems on those walls and

ceilings already drought-stricken,
one mud,
brick red, becoming another.

I have seen dying blossoms. I have brought
my one and
only love whose love is dying

nine towering daylilies the color
of persimmons.
She clips them, lets them wilt

until they are like hands or pieces of flesh
with too much
moisture on the surface.

I cannot see what fragments of light protect them.
            There is
        her garden lined with stones—she

likes them wet for their fossil markings.
            Weeps at a gift
        of flowers as heavy and weak-

necked as a month-old child.
            I can almost
        sense the child,

taste the first, sweet particles of milk . . .
            Dear reader—
        this body, *her body,* by all possible means.

Part IV

Translations from the Natural World

It gathers to a greatness, like the ooze of oil
Crushed.
—Gerard Manley Hopkins, "God's Grandeur"

On the hill beside the overpass: a single pillow toppled as if
from a passing truck-bed,
its slipcase soiled, its

railroad-striped ticking: color of owl wing, color
of semen.
I know something along this road

could be my medicine. Some bit of leaf or clutch of stalks
I could hang
by the stems

in a raw shed, then dry and crumble.
Or from the garden: a daylily
snipped

to beautiful moths in a midday soup.
Icon: *scissors.*
Icon: *one flesh, pillow, becoming*

another. Easter Sunday once, I saw three deer feeding
in an unturned field,
their singular code

overlaying the landscape until all I had was one fading
lightning strike
of inattention.

Stare harder, there are fish in the trees.
                    The leaves of the oak are swimming
          in ether. Until Michael says,

"Look, there's an egret."
                    Each dead leaf on the river
          in effortless pivot. Current under us

like Hopkins's oil (out, then back, then out again,
                    because the first time gone
          we forgot the paddles):

the river carried (*the pillow carried*)
                    as a field
          carries run-off. J-stroke, backstroke,

sidestroke. Stringed iron forming in the shoulder caps.
                    And then the boat snaking in
          to reeds and backwash.

Huge frogs hanging from hooded eyes.
                    Half-human, alligator sprawl.
          One so patiently dazzled

I could lay a fingertip upon its skull.
                    The skin: dry,
          rubbery, protective, sealed. Icon:

leaping. The feel of this leaping
                    on the car ride
          home. How these things seized us:

the anacondas of tire tread. The sticks, as heavy
as magnets,
suddenly levered into the car's undercarriage.

On a Gift of Flowers Thrown by the Wind or a Young Girl

That the wind is fierce liquid we comprehend—
evidence
in the strands of cloud

that are pushed about like feathers
against
the grain of their own webbed

passion, which is eastward;
a single, strong
powerful stream the shape

of the lake's curve (how could it
not be
otherwise?) pouring

to the west, filling our view
with
perceivable volume, holes,

where some of the cloud drops
through,
finally, like water,

whole bands of it moving
back
across the lake so that

there are at least three levels
this late
summer morning in the bundled

sky. Zones of permanence
looping
inside zones of transience—

the texture and weight of feeling
moving
over exposed skin.

We are standing, barefooted,
on
sharp, slippery stones,

wading through chilled water. Angle
of wind
through your open sleeves,

hoods billowing, my hand
in yours,
then not, then there again—

whatever flesh sings in the cold
air
as tentative as a theory

of ash or atmospheres, ropes
of wind
beside ropes and knots of

water, three children clumped
on
the near bank. They watch

our arms that are like wind, saying,
shall we dare
this thing?

Shall we, too, tiptoe over sharp rock
to feel
what is part wave swell

and part spindrift, part an invisible
whistling
the gulls acknowledge,

sailing now and then, wings spread,
thought
keening in the older child

to push the youngest near us,
a breeze
of a girl, a slip of wind

or water? . . . Now the gulls
stilled,
our arms stilled,

shall we, too, dare this thing
a child
imagines?

The sure movement in her (perceived
in us)
that is fluid, human

thought, human longing,
outside us
now—a tug

at our sleeves—the wind or the water's
silence
laying crimped flowers at our feet.

Aside

Bottom-feeding in the physical world again, I'd take this and this alone if it were all that was given—a single wasp angling out of its grained hive; thrashing sting to the belly; my body slung as if on a filament of rain . . . and the venom spreading.

Partial Glimpses of the Face of Jesus

The hand pulled back from water is always partially
gloved
with water (as the soul

must be, gazing through a river's staggered
brilliance,
cloudwork lighting the weave

of trout)—something a stiff wind
could
evaporate, or fingers leak back to the river.

The same river moving now, undulant,
before me.
Spirit infusing spirit along a rip

in gravity. Current in it like a corkscrew.
Silt riding high
on the rain's torque,

then tiring in a long, dull, nutrient curtain.
Rev-
elation swifter there for certain fish;

sunlight glossing even the spray of stones.
How could I
ever hope to contain such radiance,

another angling next to mine, touching
mine,
inside me like a coiling liquid,

a slur in the heart or blood
carried
as uneasily as word carries matter?

I know the flicker's cry now—two short bursts
of repeatable
longing—and where

the woodpecker nests, its song inside,
then
outside of the tree. A starling on a dead

limb, hovering as I hover—wanting
to steal
its home. Our attention—

the something beautiful given. As the cranes
are,
or the pepper-black gathering

of clouds. My driving parallel to the sunset
for awhile
in a blood-orange light—

radio playing—then cutting along
a backroad—
belief so rife in the fields

and yards, the cattle lie down around it,
horses
shuttle in the wind,

galloping right up to the edge of wire.
And a creek
there, too, flattened backwater,

blister of scum and weeds.
I took
two photographs near this place once

and stacked them into a single shot,
a deer's
carcass up close matching the contour

of the creek so that it was a single body
of water,
something in the pliant ribs

mirrored exactly in the pattern
of swaying
reeds. As if the animal

had paused in that last terrible
in-rush
of breath and held it there until

the truck passed and the water stilled,
and its eyes
drained of color. And then,

of course, the daylight whistling,
its long
spears marring the chamois. Torso

and water, my own body and water.
The smell
of the deer like a garment

thrown down from the afterlife . . . Somewhere
in the tall
grass, a golden bird. Mules,

in a shaded grove, as magnificent as
palominos;
a heron, I thought,

drinking from their pool, two-dimensional
at first
in the water's glazed

aspect, then suddenly alert to presence—
full-bloomed,
wide-winged. Two deer later

staring back at me from their side of this trespass.

Sequence: Turbine

(near Otto E. Eckert Station)

And so now these revolutions per second, the churning of chrome blades against the rush of steam—one hammering central thread of it. Then diffusion, residue, relay—a squirrel laid out on a limb outside my window. Its bright voicings, a chipping away as if with flint. As if each possible heavenly vector spread from this machine/animal's spin and weave. Spark and spasm. The irrefutable turbine; the sufficient branch. The body that observes this elsewhere: zones of quiet. The mind elsewhere: bird cry. Slur of wheels. Slush of wind. As if it, too, were panning for some irreplaceable element. Not this pitting and wobble: the mind (once *elsewhere*) thrown down into the body's lateral spill. Bright, beautiful cage of the senses. Train noise from across the river. Truck noise. The smear of chassis (the horn sounding now that the dam is opening—get out of the water)—one red car and then another arcing over the sunlit bridge. Doorway (*here*) thrashing like a drying towel, drying body. Oak limbs tipped with late summer leaves. Rain still clinging to their undersides (*shadow of her hand cooling cooling skin*) so that when the wind shifts, there is this narrow shower, column of wet. Spray of fingertip (*sound of the river*) along the ridge of spine. Hands fanning outward. Then pull-down. Push-back. Blades of the arms . . . O bright hair caught on the tongue again—infinitesimal spark—what light from your kinked arc strung . . .

Detail from *The Garden of Delights*

That which I cannot give I give to you: fish smell
                    from the river,
          the house of God three blocks

north: all rusted girder, dead sky,
                    the I-beams tagged
          with signature

and phosphorescence. Daily,
                    we drive past it, say
          small things, sweet

nothings. Your voice, your own,
                    in which
          an ocean

might occur . . .

*

                              In Oregon

where I held you once, there was
                    a counter-
          pulse that slipped

beneath the roll of breakers
                    and made
          a ripping sound, an X along

the shoreline. *Bosch Beach,*
we called it: tattooed lovers
everywhere, pitched

on blankets, amputees, the elderly
in the comfort
of their con-

traptions; downshore, a car tire
poked at,

*

burning; children

like half-drowned dogs, and half-
drowned
dogs, clobbered by wave

swells, hunkered on their hind legs,
wrapped
in towels, shivering—

the entire hundred yards of human/
animal flesh
stippled

with the coming chill, cold star,
my arm
in yours, the energy

along that shifting edge released and

*

ripped—a sliver,

no, spear of water. This accident
of geography,

our accident, more a matter now of will
than memory,
to be transformed

and overcome . . . *At our age,*
Williams says,
at our age, the whole process

is one of switchbacks, down
and back
across the bluff

to blinding

*

sand, water.

At the far end: three bathers, naked;
the earth
so flat between the outcrops,

gently pitched, the ocean rolls in
nearly
weightless—molten silver, air.

Sunlight: drizzle of a star. Heat we know
will
fail us in this great

middle panel:

*

we enter, disrobe, and

walk, the sea
semen-edged; sand—

that first ground—jeweled, glistening.
Fish-spirit, bird-
spirit; animal

on animal back; the kingly—
lion, panther, griffon—
driven, circling;

the egg and the owl . . .

*

At our age,

this thorn-and-thistle bath
lifts us
to make worlds of spray

and stone, lifts us (one of the bathers
strolling
now, so easily

rendered, out of the great salt room
of the sea)
to scalding air (the sky) everlasting.

Notes

"Childhood's Face": Epigraph translated by Paul Schmidt.

"A Night and a Day of Fever": Epigraph translated by Louise Varèse.

"Translations from the Natural World": For Michael Ripple.

"Detail from *The Garden of Delights*": The phrase quoted is from "The Ivy Crown" by William Carlos Williams.

About the Author

Dennis Hinrichsen earned an M.F.A. in creative writing from the University of Iowa. Currently, he teaches at Lansing Community College in Michigan. His previously published works include *Message to Be Spoken into the Left Ear of God*, *Detail from* The Garden of Earthly Delights, winner of the 1999 Akron Poetry Prize, *The Rain That Falls This Far* and *The Attraction of Heavenly Bodies.*

About the Book

Cage of Water was designed and typeset by Amy Freels Petersen, with help from Melanie Rowand.

Printed in the United States
22138LVS00003B/133-639